Literature written for young adults...

by young adults.

Allow yourself to be surprised.

What Is?

Young Writers Chapbook Series

Kaitlin Britton Wheeler

Atlanta

Copyright © 2014 by Kaitlin Britton Wheeler
Published by VerbalEyze Press

All rights reserved. Printed in the United States of America. No part of this book may be used or reproduced in any manner whatsoever, including Internet usage, without written permission from VerbalEyze Press except in the case of brief quotations embodied in critical articles and reviews.

Cover design by Ava Wong
Edited by Derek Koehl
ISBN: 978-0-9910209-6-6

VerbalEyze Press books are available at special discounts for bulk purchases in the United States by corporations, institutions and other organizations.

For information, address VerbalEyze Press, 59 Thayer Avenue SE, Atlanta, Georgia 30315.

VerbalEyze does not participate, endorse, or have any authority or responsibility concerning private correspondence between our authors and the public. All mail addressed to authors are forwarded, but the publisher cannot, unless specifically instructed by the author, give out an address or phone number.

VerbalEyze Press
A division of VerbalEyze, Inc.
www.verbaleyze.org

Table of Contents

Foreword
Editor's Note

Why I Write
Misunderstood
Dollars
Music Lesson
To Die For
What is?
Stained Concrete
Happy Father's Day
Letter to my friend's bully
I'll Be Fine
Flow
57 Shots

: What Is?

Foreword

Every teacher understands that those who love the craft are perpetual students.

While mentoring, teaching and guiding the YaHeard? Poets, I have become their student venturing to type poems into smart phones and opening my mind to Instagram as a viable canvas. They want to keep me current. And I still insist that they meditate on Rilke's *Letter to Young Poets* and put pen to paper every now and then because this is an exchange of ideas.

As we explored the many ways to express our place in the world, we realized that word and art were beautifully intertwined so we made room at the table and became the YaHeard? Art Collective. The name was simply a formality. Young artists avail themselves of every art form as they test and train their unique voice to ask the questions, challenge the status quo and confirm their presence as artists on the come-up.

So it is my honor to introduce the aspiring photographers and visual artists who dared to illustrate the growing pains their counterparts recorded. Each art form confirmed the other as the writers marveled at being understood and the artists beamed at being able to interpret what was unspoken. This is certainly the beginning of a beautiful friendship.

And this collaboration is what the art community is all about. Come and see for yourself what has been sketched, narrated, painted and poeted.

Whether speaking heartache at the mic, spitting social commentary over tracks or texting observations into the ether, the power and influence of word is undeniable and the

YaHeard? Art Collective studies the craft, explores the creative process and revels in collaborations with organizations like VerbalEyze—a beacon for young artists.

YaHeard? was founded by Educator-Artists to support the creative stirrings of tweens and teens and the publication of this chapbook honors and encourages the work of a young artist whose passion and talent confirms them as part of a new generation of prolific writers, artists and photographers.

Open your heart, ready your mind and take note. The teacher is ready to begin.

Ya Heard?

Susan Arauz Barnes
Co-founder
YaHeard? Art Collective

Editor's Note

VerbalEyze Press exists as an extension of VerbalEyze's simple mission to develop the next generation of great authors and provide those young authors with a platform from which they can share their vision and passion.

The Young Writers Chapbook Series is an expression of this mission and vision that is core to what we do at VerbalEyze. Through this series, we are able to introduce talented, emerging young authors to the reading public.

We are grateful that you also share an enthusiasm for young authors and the vibrant and energized perspectives they bring to our shared understanding of the human experience. Despite their young age, they speak with insight as to what it means to live, long, love, lose and wonder as we travel through this world.

With this edition of the Young Writers Chapbook Series, we are pleased to bring to you *What Is?*, the début publication of an exceptional young writer, Kaitlin Britton Wheeler. We trust that you will be as engaged and challenged by her words as we have been. Kaitlin is part of an exceptional group of young writers, YaHeard? Art Collective. She and her fellow writers are an never-ending encouragement and inspiration to us.

Read, enjoy and, as always, *allow yourself to be surprised*.

Derek Koehl

I want to thank everyone who believed in me even before I believed in myself.

Why I Write

These emotions are hurting me
Holding me back from opportunity
Fearful to be
Too blind to see
That I hold the key
To my emotions
Unnecessary mind commotion
Trying to figure out how to hold this
So I grab the pad, bottle up my emotions
Pour them on the paper, watch it flow, and
Use it to my advantage because I know

It's keeping me in
So I gotta let it go

What Is?

Misunderstood

Wrapping your mind around this topic is complicated
Sat back, silent as we contemplated
Our generation being annihilated
Young girls constantly violated
Young boys, gang affiliated
While we watch, humiliated
Young girls act fast
Try to run away from a lost past
From a father who couldn't last
Can't stand to feel outcast
Trying to provide for a fatherless kid
Wanted love, so that's what she did
Young boys desire connection
A real sense of protection
Gang banging, end up in corrections
Or dying over a meth injection
Deal dope on the corner block
Come off tough, hard as rock
Yet inside these boys yearn but don't talk
And to this I give great dedication
Speaking for a misunderstood generation

Kaitlin Britton Wheeler

Dollars

Dollars, great men, good looks. **Dollars**
Buy great books. **Dollars**
For the ones who got shook. **Dollars**
For the convict, for the crook. **Dollars**
For the innocent who can't get off the hook. **Dollars**
For the girls he gave dirty looks. **Dollars**
For the innocence he took. **Dollars**
Don't make you a good man, and it ain't a good look

What Is?

Music Lesson

Class is now in session
Teaching this generation
Music through time
Get ready for this lesson

FIRST
Shipped in shackles
Black women, children, and men
Iron hoes in hand, and
Steady calling work songs
To keep from dying inside
Hoe Emma Hoe
Emma help me
When will I be free?
Hard metal clinks
Like gospel tambourines
Singing: No more, my Lawd

SECONDLY
March together to end separation
Feet steady, hands joined
Humming their hymns
As the church bells ring
Shouting through the streets

Kaitlin Britton Wheeler

"We shall overcome
Oh deep in my heart I do believe
We shall overcome someday"

THIRDLY
Black bodies swingin'
In the summer breeze
Strange fruit hangin'
From the poplar trees
Strangled and left
Red blood drips
Hang still, lifeless
Billie Holiday tells the story
A mere experience
The pastoral scene of the gallant South
Meditation on Strange Fruit

FOURTH
Ready to revolutionize
DJs with opinions
"I'm ready and hyped plus I'm amped
Most of my heroes don't appear on no stamps"
Seen as the Public Enemy
Spit powerful rhymes
For the black community
To fight the power

What Is?

TODAY
Popular ignorance
Influences a generation
"I can make cocaine
I just feel in love with a Cuban"
Foreign sense, nonsense
Iconic turned corrupt
"I'll beat it up like Emmett Till"
Sick beat and ill lyric
Do you understand me?
Class is dismissed

Kaitlin Britton Wheeler

To Die For

Perfectly chiseled cheeks
Body like she'd been pumping iron for weeks
Polished plastic legs strolling on the floor
Man, she's got a figure to die for!
But is that what she died for?
Because she has pretty plump cheeks
A well-kept body for weeks
Healthy thick legs amble on the floor
Yes, that is what she died for
She was a scholar, intelligence beyond compare
Nice, thick; flowing hair
Earned a full scholarship to Columbia
Said her body was too large to be a model,
She submitted to anorexia
Without sustenance for a few months at a time
Posed for the camera, not even paid a dime
As long as the boys admired her body style
She kept deciding not to eat for a while
Lost her scholarship, no longer respected at school
Yet she was fine as long as she looked good posing by the pool
After a while she could feel the pain
Tied the rope to the fan,
Never took a beautiful breath again

What is?

Is my life too much of a luxury
That I cannot truly understand?
What is a world without a helping hand?
In a split second, life can be taken
Now, can you decipher the point I'm makin'?
A boy shot dead on the nearby street
How is a child supposed to live in this heat?
Ain't nobody too focused on this life
If it's too short to live
This ain't nothing new
We won't be surprised when the gun is on you
It wasn't an argument, a conflict, strife
He just don't like you kid
Bang!
That's just life.

Kaitlin Britton Wheeler

Stained Concrete

We walk blindly on the concrete
Stained with the blood of a boy who dreamed
Of becoming an investigator
But he became the crime scene

We walk blindly on the red concrete
Missing the eyes of a boy who was only 16
Now blood-covered and stricken
Too deaf to hear his scream

We walk blindly on the red concrete
Our youth struck down on his knees
His face remembering
Feeling the summer breeze

We continue to walk blindly on his hardened blood
Not stopping because it's just another 1 dead
Won't pause to fully recognize
That the concrete is still stained red

What Is?

Happy Father's Day

Hey Father, it's me!
The daughter you left fatherless at three
The one you left broken hearted
When you didn't see what you started
You were needed and never there
From the times I missed you
To the times I didn't care
Lonely in an empty driveway
Waiting to see you again someday
Momma, covering the tears in her eyes
Shading her pain from your lies
Devastated by these break ups
Because no one will ever makeup
The hole you left deep in my heart
Even when you left, not one goodbye
You were a coward who couldn't provide
So you left a mother and child alone
Yet we've stayed strong, fine; fending on our own
So Happy Father's Day and thanks to you
I know what not to do

Kaitlin Britton Wheeler

Letter to my friend's bully

Dear Bullies,
I've got a friend
Hooked to IV's
A girl on the edge
Her beauty gashed by lies
When nobody saw the tears in her eyes
She submitted to your words
Responded with razor cuts
Her wrist split in thirds
Found her lifeless
Remembering
"You don't belong here
Your best bet is in the grave
Where no one can see you"
Blood drained in the tub
Bathing unconscious, death scrub
Her lifeless eyes screamed to me
Hopeless, she yearned to be set free
Rushed to the hospital
Laying on the gurney
She can only think
Why am I so ugly?
Lonely and broken
Why live to be me?

What Is?

My one and only sincere friend
Your words, the balance of living and the end
All the lies you told her
Are just a reflection of you
So when you look in the mirror
Is what you are telling other's true

Kaitlin Britton Wheeler

I'll Be Fine

Sleeves pulled up
belt wrapped tight on my bicep
It don't cause no harm
Needle to my arm
Crushed meth in my nose
Because it feels too good
Popping pills every day and night
And from everything I've seen on TV
I know it'll be alright
I might not look as good as I feel
And all of this good feeling could never be real
But as long as I have my dope
Life is no problem, I can cope

What Is?

Flow

Trying to grasp her power
Sleek like metal
Gently, she moves
Oh, so swiftly
She grants my first real skill
My thoughts remembered through her
Small enough to pocket
She holds memory
Can't do without her
Through her I speak

Kaitlin Britton Wheeler

57 Shots

50 bullets loaded into an unjust gun
19 shot dead
1 out of 3 men
Some for the friend
Some for the would be husband
So all that's left is the fatherless daughter
And the would be wife

1 young man, age 17
Yearns for some skittles and a drink
But his black skin proves suspicion
Another supposed self defense position
Followed to his rear door
1 young man, 1 bullet
Our young lie lifeless
All for going to the convenience store

High school graduate
But a black man
Must have been robbin'
Must have been suspect
Could have been college student
But to dark skinned for living
Hands shot up in surrender
The gun shots enter his body
In plain sight
But there's nobody
To speak up
Because they're all too afraid to speak

What Is?

Time to realize
That the cassette tape of injustice
Is getting to sound annoying
Can't let another bullet
Hit a black body unfairly
another black son, husband, scholar
buried 6 feet deep
in our American soil

Kaitlin lives in Atlanta, Georgia and started writing poetry at the age of nine. She was heavily inspired by artist, Billie Holiday, who taught her the value of words and the influence it has on people. She comes from a family of musicians, so she is very passionate about the arts.

Inspired by writing stories with her mother, Kaitlin loves to become what she writes. She was taught to embrace her imagination to best express herself. She plans to become an English teacher, so that she can teach her students the power of words.

Photo credit: Susan Arauz Barnes

VerbalEyze Press

Empowering young writers to say, **"I am my scholarship!"**

Open call for submissions to the *Young Writers Anthology*!

See your work in print!

        Become a published writer!

                Earn royalites that can help you pay for college!

VerbalEyze Press is accepting submissions from young adult writers, ages 13 to 22, in any of the following genres:

- poetry
- short story
- song writing
- play writing
- graphic novel
- creative non-fiction

For submission details, visit
www.verbaleyze.org

VerbalEyze serves to foster, promote and support the development and professional growth of emerging young writers.

Writers Cooperative

VerbalEyze is a nonprofit organization whose mission is to foster, promote and support the development and professional growth of emerging young writers.

The Young Writers Chapbook Series is published as a service of VerbalEyze in furtherance of its goal to provide young writers with access to publishing opportunities that they otherwise would not have.

Fifty percent of the proceeds received from the sale of the Young Writers Chapbook Series are paid to the authors in the form of scholarships to help them advance in their post-secondary education.

For more information about VerbalEyze and how you can become involved in its work with young writers, visit www.verbaleyze.org.

www.ingramcontent.com/pod-product-compliance
Lightning Source LLC
Chambersburg PA
CBHW070047070426
42449CB00012BA/3175